AF878801

FINISHING LINE PRESS
www.finishinglinepress.com

Imprecise Perishing

New Women's Voices Series, No. 135

poems by

Alexandra Barylski

Finishing Line Press
Georgetown, Kentucky

Imprecise Perishing

New Women's Voices Series, No. 135

Copyright © 2017 by Alexandra Barylski
ISBN 978-1-63534-229-1 First Edition
All rights reserved under International and Pan-American Copyright Conventions. No part of this book may be reproduced in any manner whatsoever without written permission from the publisher, except in the case of brief quotations embodied in critical articles and reviews.

ACKNOWLEDGMENTS

"Via Negativa" first appeared in *Phoebe* 45.2 as a finalist for the Greg Grummer Poetry Award.
"In Praise of Broken Men" and "Conversations & Unbelief" first appeared in *Minerva Rising* 10 for the themed issue on fathers.

Publisher: Leah Maines

Editor: Christen Kincaid

Cover Art: Maylee Wolf

Author Photo: Allyn Stott

Cover Design: Maylee Wolf

Printed in the USA on acid-free paper.
Order online: www.finishinglinepress.com
also available on amazon.com

Author inquiries and mail orders:
Finishing Line Press
P. O. Box 1626
Georgetown, Kentucky 40324
U. S. A.

Table of Contents

Plum Island Conspiracy

At Long Island's end there is a pinched kidney,
sandy question mark floating in the sound
bearing liseran drupes and conspiracies diffused
on Trade Winds past the lighthouse over tidal waters.

Hoof and Mouth was brought here, thought solvable,
thought a plague unlike anything Old Testament.
Disease is an ancient wrath—uncontained outside
man's laboratories or within. Secrets will leak.

White science, those robes that couldn't keep
us safe. These priests of our future were divining
in microbes and pathogens, perfecting man
and methods for peace: a synonym for war.

Small gods will have sacrificial slaughter—all
livestock were slain on two occasions
while ticks were turned a million dirty needles
and kept breeding in and out of cages.

Questions

Did you know that you look like that girl
on National Geographic with yellow-green eyes?

Yes. You are not the only person to peer
over-long into a place where we did not invite you.

How should I reply to this—compliment?
Each gaze reduces me, a little less of who I am.

What are you? Are you where she is from?
I want to say that I am only myself,

learning myself like a new language,
accepting bullet points about how my organs fail

me like any sign in an imperfect system,
like cranberries out of season, like friendships

promised to span America's heartland, coast to coast.
What does living with this illness mean? Which I take

to mean: How can I assure you nothing
between you and me will alter, falter

under new weight like tight soil loosed
after heavy rains or shift imperceptibly apart,

lost Pangaea, identities drifting into new shapes?
Have you seen the recent photo of that once girl?

Yes. Sharbat Gula—sea-fierce, beautifully
self-righteous with the pride of one at war,

not with herself, but with everyone
and everything attempting to erase her.

Doctor Says Something Like

imagine

    your body ivied

each night

    house grown over

stressed out beams

    hinges weakening

interminable roots

    thickly creeping tendrils

i’m thinking

    they grow for my neck

learn not to choke

    each morning

without hope

    of healing

cope

    ease into what is

new and then normal

learn slow

to property manage

a dilapidating body

weak-jointed leaning

into light

1951, Henrietta Lacks

I
Pieces of herself
scalpeled by a doctor
without consent—

cervical tumor cells
like beads clustering
in pink pearl water
of a child's toy,
those liquid tubes
we imagined were condom skins
slipped over dirty fingers,
unending
thin plastic pulled
inside itself:
outer made inner,
inner made outer—

continue to live.

No scientists understand
exactly *why*.

II
White men reproduce
this black woman
for pride, for profit,
for scientific pleasure,
turn her body into myth:
immortal,
everlasting,
invariably rising

and raising white men
nearly dead. Cells
enslaved as a body's healer
when no one could heal
her.

III
HeLa cells,
one helluva cell for polio vacs
growing culture petri dish stacks,
first space mission
with zero gravity and back—
take note on those
and these facts of her
in a world where facts
are never neutral
no matter what a doctor tells you.

IV
Twenty-five years later,
a researcher telephoned
Henrietta's widowed husband,
and with his 1950's
Jim Crow education he hears:

We've got your wife.
She's alive in a laboratory.
We've been doing research
on her for the last 25 years.
We want to test your kids
to see if they have cancer.

V

Me and he are leveled
when my white-coated doctor,
sterile god (unreachable)
tells me to read potential
healing procedures:

phospholipids are amphiphilic lipids…
can reduce CIRs response in a body…
all cell death is instantaneous
after a break in the membrane…

My desire is consensual
healing for these cells—
my doctor's inanimate,
anonymous facts,
vacuoles of my self
cased in a frangible body.

But there is no *yes*
if I lack understanding
and do not know
what my own doctor
might experiment.

Via Negativa

A mouth knows shapes for certain dying.

Says *lunulas*
grey-bluing like whites
unseparated on laundry day.

Murmurs *knees*
violaceous mottling, plum over
stone of cartilage and bone.

Whispers *spine*
blood pooling, thick-foamed
like a red sea at the sacrum.

Sighs *chest*
heart open last exhale, slow breath
swan dive, elsewhere unveiled.

My doctor's mouth discloses
illness is not an assured shape.

Not start and finish, nothing marked or measured,
familiar like *Tocatta and Fugue in D Minor* ending
in a plagal cadence, definitive musical *Amen.*

Not sea-drifted storm wreckage washed up tattered,
no pretending to be wholly whatever china cup,
beer bottle, water glass life it lived before.

Not a magnolia's petioles cupping broad-lipped flowers
oyster white, steady browning, wilted greens
shriveled, petals yellow-fleshed ending.

Not clear sloped decay of decomposition,
apricots time-lapsed displaying flesh's
singular route to purification.

My mouth seeks contours
for imprecise perishing.

My lips mouth at blue air in silence wanting
what will not be given a sensible frame,
an intelligible container, an architecture of *is*.

Side Effects of Marriage I

No longer a body. Yes body. Only a body
that does no splits over his legs or opens over
and over for him to take what weeks keep out
of reach. She is an unapproachable distance.
They are stars, bright and agitated, remote
from one another as they are visible. He burns
as she burns out. Unfair how she's out-stripped him,
living spent before she knew she was running
out of green like Hemingway claims we bankrupt:
slowly, then all at once there is nothing to hold.
Hold her a little longer though she makes contact
unendurable, like a sprint with no promise of a finish.
Are they finished? In sleep, she nightmares you leave me,
always a different door, which doesn't matter—
you walk out and away from a body resembling mine.

Diagnosis: Restrictions Apply

Like pulling a stubborn sticker from its paper place,
nails working sticky edges while eyes stay steady,
I finger open his gesture: turkey, cheddar cheese, tomato.

Alone in a library garden, no one sees my practice.
I peck-pull out the middle like a bird tugging
at centers of dew-glued mown grass balls.

Sides laid back together, I re-wrap cheese slicked bread
in waxy tan butcher paper, which appears full (whole half
of sandwich) I am not to drop for courtyard birds.

I touch recovered bread and cheese, recall uncovered skin
and salt—my bird bones light, hard-pressed around sureness
of a boy's solid self. Once I was whole and wholly becoming.

Luna Park, Coney Island 1940's

Falcate moons positioned like ink
drawn curves of a woman's breasts,
another flipped to form

a crescentic arched entrance,
two like single quotation marks
with no words between them or Pisces

placed fin to head. Witness 250,000 lights
illume a night in no need of its natural
heavenly mirror, perlaceous sliver of orb.

Electric Eden, a world new with excess
where science speaks fantasies and fictions
into flesh under incandescent tungsten filaments.

Here, hearts are permitted to subjugate
what does not imitate and voyeur bodies
who are born to misbehave and can not obey,

which is another container to say: *here is a place*
for people science has not yet solved
There was Monkey Girl, whose hair grew

everywhere and married Alligator Boy,
whose skin greyed and scaled with ichthyosis.
Spider Boy learned to swing his crippled legs

from branch to branch spinning
filaments of fear and astonishment.
Babies small enough hold in a single hand

were kept like yellow chicks in every school
incubated from eggs into less abstract forms:
no longer albumen, yolk, chalazae, and shell.

But what did the teacher do with those
that never warmed enough to hatch, with lives
who needed a little more time but were denied?

Was there no classroom sideshow that might save
these almost hatchlings like Dr. Courney's
amusement park exhibit of incubator babies,

those preemies, like his own daughter, whom doctors
agreed would never survive in an advancing world?
Gawkers' pennies paid for constant care mothers

could not afford and hospitals would not allow.
Discarded humans with nowhere to go found
a congregation on Coney Island, *Narrioch*,

Lanape's *land without shadows*, seashores *always in light.*
Light of moons, heat of electric suns, warmth of belonging
incubate us as we wait for answers in our unsolvable bodies.

Lustrum

The priest will order one of two birds
    to slaughter over a clay pot of fresh water.

Borrelia burgdorferi spirochetes, winged demons, flutter
    through this body, build nests between vertebra

like a parakeet's deadly cousin, more lustrous—
    my lucent bacteria fowls.

The priest commands: Gather a juniper branch
    stripped of gin bearing berries;

coccus wool, yarn dyed scarlet by a female worm,
    a mother's blood;

hyssop before it blooms and yields oblong archenes;
    cradle-palm the living

bird filled with evensong. Build my aspergillum.
    Bind songbird and hyssop

to juniper branch with crimson twine,
    tail feathers fanning radiant with fear.

Dip her hollow bones and clean heart
    into my clay pot lustral mixture.

Seven aspersions. Unbound spirit,
    songbird fly away my demons—

illness leaving a body.
    Maybe this rite will not cure me.

But I was permitted participation,
    given an articulate world—

bird, plant, worm, water, blood.
    O nameable world, my rite,

let these curved fingers cling
    to a sayable world and save me.

Knocking for a Miracle

"God does not provide or promise divine healing for those
who want to live in sin." —a sermon I heard

God the Son was busy about his own business,
taking compassion on a blind man cursed
since birth with the dark seal of his mother's
alleged indiscretions (to say nothing of his own).
And what about a woman, bowed together,
whom Jesus called to himself—no questions asked,
no interrogation of faith or proclamation a confession
had worked to make her stand up, righteous, whole.
In Jerusalem down by a sheep market there is a pool
where a man who, crippled thirty eight years, waited
a season for an angel who would trouble those waters.
But his trouble was how to enter where no others—
all too centered on healing themselves—were willing
to carry his soft curling body, like so many petals, into a bath.
The Son of God only asked if he wanted to be made unbroken,
demonstrating desire is enough to save—an avidity,
an ache, an appetite for restoration is all recovery requires.

God the Father is busy leading ideologies of men
from the comfort of his own home.
When she knocks at his door in her Sunday dress,
she announces that she longs to see his shut-in son,
his only one, broken hearted little lamb.
Like other fathers, his body blocks her
from entering, scans her, makes it clear she is not a girl
who would give his son a good name.

Difficult to say which of them was more disappointed:
the son who nearly died knowing he was forsaken by his father;
the father who refused to learn how to comprehend his son;
or her breaking-down body in perfect want of a miracle.

In Praise of Broken Men

for the day laborer, for the sick man

Have you seen them on damp mornings when autumn's cold slides her wet fingers beneath each of their labor-stained layers? Have you seen their trucks lined up outside gas station convenient stores, idling exhaust pluming like their holiday cigars? Have you seen their flat-beds loaded with licorice root mulch, contractor bags, shovels, rakes, clippers: tools for taming, shaping, growing the land? Have you seen their fraying bodies, aged beyond their ages, broken daily for their family's bread?

My father moved with them— ill, still undiagnosed, work-tanned, pain-creased, and shuffling toward his truck's door, silent with his nose deep inside a paper cup of dollar coffee, his mind deep inside an old, Polish prayer.

I have seen you wrinkle your nose in line behind his rotten-egg smell, blessèd potency of earth ready to return to nourish earth. I have seen you watching him, suspicious he might steal, as if he is not a holy man among you, caretaker of our dirt and ditch world. I have seen wonder cross your face: *This man in his holey camouflaged jumpsuit and soily skullcap at the coffee counter must be homeless.*

Remember with me. Remember how, when I was five, a woman hovered over us as I ordered my pork roll, egg, and cheese before school. Was I supposed to be with you, she wanted to know. (Whom else should I have been beside?) Remember my perfect adoration—how I rushed to grab your dirty, swollen hand—my small love clinging to one of three bodies broken for me.

Grain of Us

Slope of ligneous flesh
                    my adolescent arms
felt sp lit
          and
                    fall
                              of kindling
absorbed shocks
                    dividing

          each log's denseness down its middle

throb and thrill of power
                    in my uncalloused hands

Happiness was clefting   this world

that left
        his body riving,
                        dry lumber for blazing

My cells
                              s pl   in t er

Together we are
                              struck-split

grain of us
                              indefensible

di
  vided by our shared ax

                              burning

Apologia Pro Vita

He is a man who claims there is only one way to live
in slow motion dying: argument

Grass slimmed and yard gave way to hostas, black-eyed Susan's, lamb's ear, chamomile, rosemary, parsley, thyme, cucumbers, and eggplant. Even now, in the right season, clematis drapes a porch surrounded by geraniums.

Salvia stands tall near a back door, and his beloved Japanese irises bloom in a far corner of the yard. Daylilies never fail to wake in their beds.

Memories ivy an east side fence.

See honey suckle and trumpet vines trained over bric-a-brac and ponds he built for a woman's strange goldfish. Examine butterfly and hummingbird bushes.

See, some small life is always in need of his care.

Note his pastel-shaded plea, brilliant jeweled defiance, evergreen justification for a body doing anything
but blossoming in his inflorescent world.

His *caritas* is a soft madness, a gracious lunacy—mania of a thousand peony heads disputing his right
to stay on this dirt.

Conversations & Unbelief

I have been talking to Jesus, postcards my father.
So I know his ears are leaning to bloodroot, anemone wood, spice bush,
and Rose of Sharon. God grows wild in my father's cemetery garden

where he kneels, hired-hand, between interned ashes
and cleans where our world grows weedy or throws
candy-wrapper trash after love-making on mossy beds.

I can not decide if this act desecrates or celebrates the dead,
whom I love sitting among and walking beside because
they share my dark laughter. My father is a dying man

tending flowers surrounding the dead. He is my own Father Zossima
telling me faith is only found in subjective acts of love, ministry of annual
and perennial, root and stem, stamen and petal, pruning discernment—

My father knows three languages: Silence. Anguish. Flowers.
He uses two and speaks to people who want to hear him. Lately, I am not
that person who will listen:

Life will bring you many misfortunes, but you will find your happiness in
them, and you will bless life and will make your life a blessing for others—
which is what matters most.

Daughters are not permitted to understand their fathers. Witness
his strange gladness, which is unassailable under an open sky, surrounded
by someone's dead, listening for healing words in flowers.

Learning to Worship

All our lives   are narrated by leaving.

Sooner or later

we must anoint a body   bless it with tears like Mary

perfuming time   with pending loss.

O my beloved I will   Spikenard my hair

whose split-tips touch

sick-slimmed hips   all bone   when my head   is tilted

by something like laugher.

Throw   fistfuls   of mercy

blue corn   rice   rose petal confetti—

give what takes   time growing

costs belly and eyes nourishment

and pop   a bottle of red   not champagne

blood   not bubbles.

Worship   is not equivalent   to praise.

Only one is demanding

teaches   you   how to hold loss

soft-bodied   holy.

Darning

A patch for holes not running along seams:
splits whose healing will remain visible.
Here is where I scarred my knee skateboarding.
There is the elbow burn from afterschool asphalt.
If only my mother could stitch my unseen gash,
weave weft through warp and repair me.
I take her wooden darning gourd, painted black lacquer,
press its ovoid head against my flattening belly—
intestines and stomach no long dangerously enflamed
from any small thing: a little sugar, some wheat.
Fingers move over my abdomen as if I want
to pulp out what never fruited, never will.
There is no provisional patch-up for a psychic tear:
slim chance for a thread from me to some small you.

Side Effects of Marriage II

Stand before dirty dishes, olive oil
ringed crockery, and butter slicked
cutlery sunken to an unseen bottom.
The same knife waits to cut—

Alone with life's knuckle-swell,
a sigh before this washing,
which is somehow more labor
than friend, lover, family fed.

If there is recovery, let it be
cookware's continuous renewal,
this cleanliness required for pots
to brim with sustenance again.

In daily soaping, soaking,
scrubbing away of garlic, grains,
and root is a world that anchors
life and offers assurance

in rote, in repetition, in remembrance,
in toning practical practices—
love's muscled memory
moving bodies (almost) forward.

Trust in unconsciousness:
off key humming *Moon River,*
a blitzed *I'm so sorry,*
two hands toweling dishes.

Efflorescence

Flowering   crystalline deposits

water's evaporation

white stain
stalactites dripping

bricks breaking
into mineral blossoms

Imagine organs

saltpetered
like this wall

or spangled

as this student's
black notebook

methodical white-out

fractal galaxy
stars
and hearts
forever

Don't give
a damn
why intestines leak toxins

how science explains any body

Dream
the figure interior

anatomy cavernous

icicled
in pink
and green salt

or as a girl's unruly
constellation

each heart
beat budding

into
heavy-petaled
stars

Healing Prophecy

For days when skeletons lie in the Valley of Dry Bones.

For hours when tendon, tissue, and skin are exiled.

For moments when dryness forgets how to dream of rain.

Remember fullness presses close in particles
and waves of light, which illumes

cranberries in the bog and young blueberries
on the stem (their damson the color of winter lips).

Every purple is the color of humility,
is a god who rushes to kiss you now.

Cold apples, wild strawberries, a creek-side iris,
jasmine in full bloom. At night
the word *lush* will enter the air, your mouth.

Maybe

I would guzzle a pint of bleach
if I thought it would heal
this carbon-based body
eating, drinking, loving, hating
its relentless submission
to laws of matter—
immedicable
insides immune to nothing;
yet, it seems better to feel
forever blessed,
breakable miracle
walking without protection:
all my Wednesdays write me with ash,
mark me sinew, tissue, bruisable—
whole human.

Alexandra Barylski is fascinated by the exuberance and exhaustion of the body. Her poetry appears or is forthcoming in *Ninth Letter, Ruminate Magazine, Phoebe, Minerva Rising, Ithaca Lit,* and elsewhere. She won the 2015 Morton Marcus Poetry Prize. She was a finalist for the 2016 Fairy Tale Review Poetry Prize and the Yemassee Journal Poetry Prize. She participated in Tupelo Press' 30/30 project for National Poetry Month, 2017. This is her first chapbook.

CPSIA information can be obtained
at www.ICGtesting.com
Printed in the USA
LVHW01s1624010418
571876LV00011B/666/P

9 781635 342291